# Beyond
# Slavery

# Beyond Slavery

## The Northern Romantic Nationalist Origins of America's Civil War

### Walter Kirk Wood

SHOTWELL PUBLISHING
Columbia, South Carolina

Produced in the REPUBLIC OF SOUTH CAROLINA by

SHOTWELL PUBLISHING, LLC
Post Office Box 2592
Columbia, South Carolina 29202

www.ShotwellPublishing.com

Cover Image: "Yankee doodle 1776 "Contributor: Clay, Cosack & Co. - Willard, Archibald M. - Ryder, James F., 1876. | Courtesy LOC.gov
Cover Design: Hazel's Dream / Boo Jackson TCB

ISBN: 978-1-947660-75-5


10 9 8 7 6 5 4 3 2 1

# CONTENTS

# FOREWORD

I know of no historian who matches Professor Kirk Wood in comprehensive research on the great questions of American history. His magisterial two-volume *Nullification: A Constitutional History* is definitive about how Americans understood our Constitution before it was perverted from the federal union that it intended into a charter of an eternal, unappealable centralized power.

Professor Wood has now taken on an equally important and distorted question—the role of slavery in bringing on the great bloodletting of 1861—1865. The old propaganda charge that the war was "caused by" slavery now dominates "expert" opinion with almost totalitarian rigour. But in his exhaustive research into this question, to be published as a three-volume *Beyond Slavery*, Dr. Wood will make a courageous refutation of that interpretation. He will show how the war became inevitable only because Northern society was infected by the revolutionary romantic nationalism that rocked Europe in the mid- 19th century. The South remained loyal to the old American dispensation of classical republicanism, and thus had to be eliminated. It was not the South's defense of slavery but the dominant North's determination to redefine America that made conflict "irrepressible."

The North's determination was rationalised by an interpretation of the Founding Fathers that redefined them as abolitionists and organic nationalists. Thus the South's constitutional and moral position could be portrayed as a rebellion against the Fathers and a threat to the patrimony. This was the opposite of the truth. Lincoln had it both ways, claiming he was preserving the sacred old Union and at the same time presiding over a "new birth of freedom."

Wood reveals to us, chapter and verse, the real Founding Fathers and how they were distorted and falsified in the 19th century. Shotwell Publishing is proud to make available this anticipatory preview to the coming masterwork, *Beyond Slavery*.

Clyde N. Wilson

# INTRODUCTION

The little book presented here is about a big topic in American history, our Civil War that was always about much more than slavery alone, either its defense on the part of the South or its abolition on the part of the North. Slavery, like many other issues dividing Americans in the nineteenth-century—banking, internal improvements, the tariff, land policy, railroads— reduced to a question of Constitutional authority. In the end, the nature of the Constitution and the government it created was the real over-riding issue. Either the American government was limited and a federal union of the states or it was not.

Southerners, along with their Northern allies, consistently maintained and defended the former view from 1789 to 1860. The ideas of a national government with unlimited powers and an indissoluble union were inventions of the nineteenth century, derived from the mixing of Romantic perfectionism with nationalism, which established a new nation as a "New birth of Freedom."

Slavery may have been abolished legally in 1865, but black freedom was yet to be achieved. For Lincoln and the Republicans, the legal abolition of the ownership of humans as property satisfied their moral requirements. As free labor, blacks were now on their own to bargain for their wages. Free labor, of course, would benefit by a Protective Tariff that promised higher wages for workers as it also benefitted the business and industrial interests of the North. Republican hegemony was to be maintained, so the party of Lincoln could make permanent the economic legislation enacted during the war while the South was out of the Union— a national banking system and paper money, a tariff that continued to increase after 1865, a Homestead Law, and railroads to the Pacific, among others.

Regrettably, the motto of the new Republican party of 1854-1860, "Free Soil, Free Labor, and Free Men," was also a racist one, meaning no blacks in the territories, slave or free. This policy continued after 1865 under a new name: "Reconstruction," designed to keep the black people down South after abolition. By governing the Southern states with black voters led by "Carpetbaggers" and "Scalawags," Republicans would exact revenge against the South while assuring their party dominance.

In the bigger picture of American history from the Revolution to the Civil War, the real contest of ideas and struggle for power was between competing views of government and society. It was between eighteenth century republicanism-federalism represented by the South and its allies, on the one hand, and nineteenth century Romanticism, on the other hand, that came to be the dominant force of the antebellum North. The irrepressible conflict was between two different Americas, one born in the 18th century and another born in the 19th century. And the War of Northern-Romantic-Nationalist origins that had to come was about much more than slavery alone. The impulse to perfectionism could not be denied.

It needs to be added that the little book presented here is part of a much larger, multivolume work in progress and entitled "Beyond Slavery: A New History for a New Nation and the Northern-Romantic-Nationalist Origins of America's Civil War, 1776-1865." Volume one is now complete, "Republicanism, The Untold History of an Idea, 1776-2016." "Volume Two: Original Intentions, North and South, 1776-1865" is almost completed. A third volume will address changes in the North that perfectionist Yankees derived from the Romantic Revolution in America from 1800 to 1860. It was not the South that embraced newer ideas or "isms" in the nineteenth century; it was the North that rejected the original republican-federalist beliefs of the founders and framers. With ideas both foreign and revolutionary, perfectionist Yankees had to invent the myths of democracy (America was born modern, democratic, egalitarian, abolitionist, and nationalist) and a "Reactionary South" (as the "Slave Power") to legitimize their radical beliefs while de-legitimizing the Southern claim to the mantle of the founding generation by defining it solely as the defense of slavery.

Walter Kirk Wood

\* \* \*

"To seek the origins of the Civil War is to range over much of the nation's early history."

"Either the American people plunged into civil war for light and transient reasons, or else the spectacular quarrel over slavery in the territories was merely the skirmish line of a larger and more fundamental conflict."

(Don E. Fehrenbacher, "Disunion and Reunion," in John M. Higham, ed., *Reconstruction of American History* [New York: Harper & Brothers, 1962], 100- 102.)

\* \* \*

"Myths and legends flourish despite the accessible bodies of factual information that contradict them." (Michael Kammen, *Mystic Chords of Memory*, 26)

"Every nation needs a mythic explanation of its own." (27)

"What people believe to be true about their past is usually more important ... than truth itself." (38-39)

"Not enough people pay attention to scholarly history. They never have, and I don't believe they ever will." (38)

\* \* \*

"The nationalists won, and their victory established as truth a pentad of fictions: 1) that the war of independence had been a united war for national independence, not for the independence of the several states; 2) that the question facing the new nation was not whether it shall have a national government, but what form that government should take ...." (Forrest McDonald, *The Formation of the American Republic, 1776-1790* [Baltimore, 1967], x.)

"Before Independence ... few Americans espoused the doctrines about to be set forth in the Declaration of Independence ....

Similarly, those who in the 1780s believed that the nation should be one instead of many had rivals in abundance ...." (ix-x)

* * *

"Under Lincoln, the United States created a national currency, powerful federal courts, and the first federal income tax. Liberty itself took on new meanings. Between 1789 and 1861, so-called negative liberty – freedom from something – permeated the national consciousness and shaped the first ten constitutional amendments, with their 'shall nots.' The Civil War brought about a shift to positive liberty, or freedom *to*. This shift was reflected in the Thirteenth, Fourteenth, and Fifteenth Amendments, which gave freedom and citizenship to millions of African-Americans in declarative phrases like "Congress shall have the power to enforce ....' Positive liberty, McPherson notes, can open the way to justice, social welfare, and equality of opportunity."

"[James] McPherson attributes the war's violence to a widely felt, passionate commitment to principle. Soldiers on both sides fought with genuine devotion to their perspective causes." (David S. Reynolds, review of McPherson, *Embattled Rebel: Jefferson Davis as Commander in Chief* and McPherson, *The War That Forged a Nation: Why the Civil War Still Matters*, in *New York Review of Books*, November 19, 2015, 41-43)

* * *

# I. A New History for a New Nation

AMERICA'S CIVIL WAR of 1861-65 was very much about 1776 and 1787 and what the founders and framers believed or not concerning slavery and many other political and economic issues. More importantly, it was about which side, North or South, was the true heir of the American Revolution and the Constitution of 1787-1788? So James M. McPherson, one of America's foremost Civil War scholars, begins his *Battle Cry of Freedom* (New York, 1988): "Both sides in the American Civil War professed to be fighting for freedom."

> The South, said Jefferson Davis in 1863, was "forced to take up arms to vindicate political rights, the freedom, equality, and State sovereignty which were the heritage purchased by the blood of our revolutionary sires." On the other side, there was the belief of Lincoln and the new Republican Party, that "if the Confederacy succeeded in this endeavor [secession] ... it would destroy the Union "conceived in Liberty" by those revolutionary sires as "the last, best hope" for the preservation of republican freedom in the world. "We must settle this question now," said Lincoln in 1861, "whether in a free government the minority have the right to break up the government whenever they choose." (vii)

Lincoln, of course, failed to note that he was a minority President with less than 40 per cent of the popular vote.

In historical terms, of course, only one side could be correct. That it was the South (and its Northern allies) who were correct rather than the North (of abolitionists, free-soilers, Lincoln, and the Republicans) is one of the contrary claims that informs *Beyond*

*Slavery*. Although McPherson sides with Lincoln and the Republicans in the end, he does so even while admitting that for a "new birth of freedom" to occur, "the Constitution written by the founding fathers" had to be transformed. Original intentions, in other words, had to be denied and replaced by much different ones.

While "Northern publicists ridiculed the Confederacy's claim to fight for freedom," and associated it with slavery not liberty, "the North did not at first fight to free the slaves." Lincoln himself had already stated that he had "no purpose, directly or indirectly, to interfere with slavery in the States where it exists." The Union Congress overwhelmingly endorsed this position in July 1861.

> Within a year, however, both Lincoln and Congress decided to make emancipation of slaves in Confederate states a Union war policy. By the time of the Gettysburg Address, in November 1863, the North was fighting for a "new birth of freedom" to transform the Constitution written by the founding fathers, under which the United States had become the world's largest slaveholding country, into a charter of emancipation for a republic where, as the northern version of *The Battle Cry of Freedom* put it, "Not a man shall be a slave." (vii-viii)

Continuing, McPherson adds:

> The multiple meanings of slavery and freedom and how they dissolved and re-formed into new patterns in the crucible of war, constitute a central theme of this book. That same crucible fused the several states bound loosely in a federal Union under a weak central government into a New Nation forged by the fires of war in which more Americans died than in all of the country's other wars combined. (viii)

As McPherson also acknowledges, a "new birth of freedom" was always about more than emancipation or abolition, given the widespread anti-black prejudice in the North even among radical abolitionists and Republicans, including Abraham Lincoln. "Free soil, free labor, and free men," after all, meant no blacks in the territories whether slave or free. "When Wilmot introduced his proviso [in 1846], he released the pent-up ire of Northern Democrats, many of whom cared less about slavery in the new territories than about political power within the party." Beyond abolitionists, the anti-slavery views of free-soilers "did not spring from a squeamish sensitiveness ... nor morbid sympathy for the slave ...." "It is not so much in reference to the welfare of the Negro that we are here [as Republicans in convention, 1856]." "I [Lincoln] am not, nor ever have been in favor of bringing about in any way the social and political equality of the white and black races...." (53, 55, 159, 186)

Speaking of the antislavery movement in general, William Gienapp, an expert on the Republican Party and Lincoln, said that both "always confronted" the "obstacle" of "Northerners' widespread hostility to blacks." "For personal and strategic reasons, Lincoln devoted little attention to the racial consequences of emancipation [as in freed slaves migration northward]." Being "an ambitious politician, he was sensitive to the power of anti-black sentiment in Illinois and frankly conceded that most whites, including himself, would not accept former slaves as political and social equals." In his own words, Lincoln said: "Whether this feeling accords with justice and sound judgment, is not the sole question .... A universal feeling well or ill-founded [sic], can not be safely disregarded." To Gienapp, "Instead of taking his usual hardheaded look at this scheme [colonization], he clung to it as a way to avoid confronting the consequences of emancipation, for which he had no solution." (*Abraham Lincoln and Civil War America*, 1992, 52.)

Writing in 1976, David M. Potter declared unequivocally that "while slavery was sectional, Negrophobia was national." About "the free-soil movement which came to overshadow the abolition movement politically in the North," Potter adds that "Instead of dealing with slaves where they were in bondage – in the Southern states – the free-soil movement, instead of proposing to free them, proposed to keep them (and free Negroes as well) out of the new areas where they might compete with white settlers." (*The Impending Crisis: America Before the Civil War, 1848-1861*, 1976, 36.)

More central than slavery to Lincoln and the new Republican Party was "a new Nation forged by the fires of war" that they sought and welcomed. "The war," McPherson writes, "marked a transition of the United States as a singular noun. The 'Union' also became the nation ...." "Before 1861 the two words 'United States' were generally rendered as a plural noun: 'the United States are a republic.'" (859) "The Union Lincoln would fight to preserve was not the bundle of compromises that secured the vital interests of both slave states and free, but was, rather, the nation – the single, united, free people" of America. The nature of the American union "was transformed between Jefferson's time and Lincoln's."

Nicholas and Peter Onuf also conclude that "Lincoln invoked Jefferson to establish a legitimating genealogy for the American nation and to define its world historical destiny." (Quoted in Gary W. Gallagher, *The Union War*, 2011, 47-48). Edward J. Blum, in "'The First Secessionist Was Satan': Secession and the Religious Politics of Evil in Civil War America" (*Civil War History*, 60 [September 2014], 234-269) admits that "This historical positioning [linking Satan to secession and the South] allowed Unionists a means to evade Confederate claims that secession followed the 'right of revolution' established by the nation's founders." (236)

For this purpose, opponents of slavery in the antebellum North had to create a "new history for a new nation in the making." Toward this end, did abolitionists, and later Republicans including Lincoln, reinterpret the principles of 1776 and 1787 to be more democratic, egalitarian, abolitionist, and nationalist than they really were? At the same time, did the South's defense of

original intentions—politically, economically, and culturally—
have to be overcome to make the Declaration more about equality
than independence and the Constitution and the union it formed
less limited and more national? Thus, the Republican propaganda
identification of the South and its Northern allies with the defense
of slavery alone to the exclusion of other beliefs and values not
slavery- related.

## REWRITING THE DECLARATION OF INDEPENDENCE

By 1860, the North-South struggle became one of *Liberty* versus *Slavery* rather than a contest between competing definitions of Liberty (19th century democracy versus 18th century republicanism) and Union (nationalist versus federal). The failed revolutions in Europe of 1848-1852 would prove to be crucial in the process of Northern-Romantic-perfectionist-nationalist myth-making—with the necessary corollary of a menacing "Slave Power Conspiracy" that threatened free labor in the North directly. (See among many other studies, Timothy Roberts, *Distant Revolutions: 1848 and the Challenge to American Exceptionalism*, 2009, and Wood," "Beyond Slavery: Reactionary South Bibliography," and "A Declaration for Independence Not Equality: Historians Tell the Truth about 1776," at NullificationHistory.com.)

Referring to Lincoln's opposition to the Kansas-Nebraska Acts of 1854 and his view that "the spirit of seventy-six and the spirit of Nebraska are utter antagonisms," Gienapp adds this qualification: "In advancing this proposition, designed to link the anti-Nebraska cause to the ideals of the founders and make it seem conservative, Lincoln simplified the Founders' record concerning slavery, which was much more mixed than he suggested." (*Abraham Lincoln and Civil War America*, 2002, 51.)

Besides Professors McPherson, Nicholas and Peter Onuf, and Blum quoted above, greater credence is afforded the Southern view of 1776 and 1787 by a Northern scholar's definitive study of America's Declaration of Independence and what it meant originally versus what it became later. In *American Scripture: Making the Declaration* of *Independence* (New York, 1997), Pauline Maier affirms that the Declaration was more about independence and justifying a right of revolution than proclaiming the equal rights of all men universally. "As a statement of political philosophy, the Declaration of Independence was therefore purposely unexceptional."(xvii) By contrast, "Lincoln's view of the past ... was a product of political controversy, not research, and his version of what the founders meant was full of wishful suppositions." (206)

In 1776 and into the early 19th-century, the understanding of the Declaration of Independence was confined to explaining and justifying political separation from Great Britain (a "painful decision" by "reluctant revolutionaries"). Informed by "convictions and emotions ... well defined in English history and tradition," only later did the Declaration become viewed in terms of "what we ought to be." This other and lesser known story of the Declaration of Independence, beyond its "original making," was about "its remaking" and has relevance to the Civil War era. Between 1815 and 1865, the Declaration became "a sacred text" and "began to assume the quasi-religious attributes later institutionalized without a shadow of subtlety." (xviii-xix) For Maier, if Lincoln did not "single-handedly" reinterpret that document by elevating equality above independence and "revolutionizing the Revolution," such thoughts "resonated" widely. (xviii, xix) Just as the original Declaration was the work of many men and not Thomas Jefferson, so too was the remaking of the Declaration "no less than its original creation not an individual but a collective act." (xix)

By 1860, in the course of many political controversies, "the document assumed a function altogether different from that of 1776; it became not a justification of revolution, but a moral standard by which the day-to-day policies and practices of the nation could be judged." (154) As a political document of extraordinary power, the Declaration was not the document of 1776 but one constructed after the fact for other uses. The second paragraph of the Declaration, "proclaims all men are created equal among many other self-evident truths about inalienable rights from their Creator for which governments are instituted among men." Prof. Maier notes that this "one long sentence . . . asserted one right, the right of revolution, which was, after all, the right Americans were exercising in 1776." Although "long essays have in fact been written on one phrase after another" from this second paragraph, "no section suffers more from a separation of parts from the whole, since its meaning lies in an escalating sequence of connected assertions."

In terms of substance, however, Jefferson's assertion of the right of revolution summarized succinctly ideas defended and explained at grater length by a long list of seventeenth-century writers that included such prominent figures as John Milton, Algernon Sidney, John Locke, as well as a host of others, English and Scottish, familiar and obscure, who continued and, in some measure, developed that 'Whig' tradition in the eighteenth century. By the time of the Revolution those ideas had become, in generalized form captured by Jefferson, a political orthodoxy whose basic principles colonists could pick up from sermons or newspapers or even schoolbooks without ever reading a systematic work of political theory. In short, and contrary to abolitionists and Lincoln and the Republicans, "the arguments Jefferson frequently expressed were . . . absolutely conventional among Americans of his time." (134-135) Those who will read Jefferson's A Summary View of the Rights of British America, which first brought him to public notice, might be surprised at his rendering of American rights entirely in the light of the British constitution.

Moreover, writes Maeir, "in none of these [other] documents [state declarations of rights] is there any evidence whatsoever that the Declaration of Independence lived in men's minds as a classic statement of American political principles. Not one revolutionary state bill of rights used the words 'all men are created equal.'" More familiar was "All men are born equally free and independent" or "All men have certain natural, essential, and inherent rights, among which are the enjoying and defending life and liberty, acquiring, possessing, and protecting property, and in a word seeking and obtaining happiness." The "pursuit of happiness" was about "life, liberty, and property." (167)

In the long controversy that preceded American independence between 1763 and 1776, one statute, the Declaratory Act of 1766, summarized all the other grievances into one operative British design and purpose that was both Parliament's and later the King's (George III) intent to "make laws that bind us IN ALL CASES WHATSOEVER" and "to enforce an unconditional submission" on the part of the colonies to the arbitrary rule of King and Parliament joined in the exercise of unlimited power in the name of sovereignty indivisible." (77-78) No more shared power between "King, Lords, and Commons"; no respect for the ancient liberties of Englishmen in America; and no desire to share power within the Empire by *imperium in imperio*.

As such, with basic rights denied, property threatened, and the means to earning a living or substance much reduced by regulations, and the "beloved continent" promising great personal and material prospects in the future to its inhabitants, the time had come at last to part ways. From Virginia came "instructions" that "the Colony had 'no alternative left but an abject submission to the will . . . of . . . overbearing tyrants, to a total separation from the Crown and Government of Great Britain.'" Similarly, did North Carolina say that "the colonies' efforts to achieve reconciliation 'on constitutional principles' had failed, and 'no hope remains of obtaining redress by those means alone which have been hitherto tried.'" In South Carolina, William Henry Drayton said about "the attempted destruction of America: 'Nature cried aloud, self-preservation is the great law; we have but obeyed.'" (83-84, 86-87).

There it was, colony-wide and in the second Continental Congress; self-preservation demanded and justified a right of revolution to begin government anew. Not a Southern thing, by any means, it was an original intention that continued to inform American political theory. "The Declaration of Independence was just one among several resolutions of the state and Continental congresses by which 'all power whatever . . . hath reverted to the people' so they could empower their representatives to 'institute and establish such a government as they shall deem best calculated to secure the rights of liberties of the good people of this State [New York].'" (163)

The Declaration, Prof. Maier informs us, also "performed a constitutional function in formally closing the previous regime." Between 1776 and 1788, colonial governments became new state ones, free and independent. To make a long story short, ancient English rights and Whig theory became Americanized as republicanism and colonial *imperium in imperio* became federalism and states' rights. To Maier, one of "the accomplishments of the Revolution" was "the federal [not national] union." (155, 187).

The Constitution of 1787-1788 (as ratified with pending amendments) created a federal government, a unique one that was no longer federal in the sense that the old Articles of Confederation were. In the new "confederate republic of a compound nature, states were sovereign within the sphere of powers reserved to them by the Tenth Amendment. The new Constitution remained a compact among the states with exclusive authority over slavery and most other matters. If not a confederacy, nor was the new government a national or "consolidated" one, in the language of the time, defined as one single government operating directly upon individuals. This was the definition of monarchy and tyranny that Americans had rejected in 1776. (See Wood, *Nullification, A Constitutional History, 1776-1833*, 2 volumes, 2008, 2009.)

As a limited and a federal government and not a national and unlimited one, in keeping with the Whig-republican principles of 1776, sovereignty resided not in the government itself but in the people of the states (not en masse or in the aggregate). Being a voluntary compact of government, following the philosophy of John Locke and other Whig theorists of the 17th and 18th centuries, a right of revolution or secession remained as the *ultimo ratio* to preserve liberty against government grown corrupt, arbitrary, and imperious. So it was believed, North and South, in America between 1776 and 1860 until denied by Abraham Lincoln and the Republicans in 1860-1861. "The concept of the Union as a rather loose association of states, each with a high degree of autonomy, was historically accurate . . . . On the central issue of slavery itself, the focus of decision was on the states" and "for several decades after the founding of the Republic, the question of slavery did not naturally become within the federal orbit." (Potter, *The Impending Crisis*, 46, 52, 52-53.)

To Paul C. Nagel, "Centralism, meaning absolute Union of one kind or another, was thus impossible in 1776 or 1787." In time, "The Union's equivocal essence was overwhelmed as the nation's consolidation routed the regional autonomy enjoyed in Jefferson's age." "Absolute Union expanded with the severity of sectional crises." "Union's transcendent version caused debate well into the nineteenth century, especially in contending that Union, being older than the Constitution, might somehow elude the constraining effect of the written word." "Finally, in behalf of the majority, Lincoln dismissed Union's theoretical character as irrelevant, thus closing an astonishing tale." (Paul C. Nagel, *One Nation Indivisible: The Union in American Thought, 1776-1861*, 1964, 4, 33-34, 44, 103, 110.)

Before the Gettysburg Address in 1863, Lincoln had already rejected the American Revolution as a *mere* war of independence.

Answering a letter from Henry L. Pierce and others on April 6, 1859, Lincoln concluded:

> All honor to Jefferson—to the man who, in the concrete pressure for *national independency by a single people* [*italics added*], had the coolness, forecast, and capacity to introduce into *a merely revolutionary document* [*italics added*] an abstract truth, applicable to all men and all times, and so to embalm it there, that to-day, and in all coming days, it shall be a rebuke and a stumbling-block to the very harbingers of re-appearing tyranny and oppression. (Don E. Fehrenbacher, ed., *Lincoln: Writings and Speeches, 1859-1865* [New York, 1989], 19.)

## IMPORTING GERMAN ROMANTICISM AND FRENCH *EGALITE'*

Lincoln and the Republicans and the abolitionists before them did indeed "revolutionize the Revolution" and the Constitution. But why this "sacralization of the Declaration of Independence" after 1815? Why its enlistment "in behalf of every cause" — the early labor movement, universal male suffrage, abolitionism, feminism, Mormonism, and more — "that might conceivably claim its authority"? Maier's conclusion (197) is that the "Declaration's new found status as a sacred document made it extremely useful for causes attempting to seize the moral high ground in public debate." Broad as it is, this conclusion does not explain why these causes emerged when they did after 1815. Nor does she identify the source of their inspiration which, obviously enough, was not the more limited and restrained Whig-republican ideology of the founders and framers!

Scholars have documented changing interpretations of the Declaration, the Revolution, the Constitution, and the nature of the union, along with how concepts such as "democracy," "equality," "liberty," and "freedom" were defined and re-defined. Yet no satisfactory explanation has been presented how or why these key concepts became so contested between different sections of the republic. The answer is to be found in the Romantic Revolution in the North (or dominant parts of that region) between 1815 and 1860. There did newer and foreign ideas or "isms" from Germanic idealistic philosophy emerge, seeking to perfect America. Manifested in Unitarianism, abolitionism, Transcendentalism, and evangelical-Arminian-latitudinarian-non-Trinitarian theology, the Northern perfectionist impulse was intent on making America anew, more egalitarian and democratic than previously. And, above all, it intended to abolish slavery.

(See most recently, Ethan Kytle, *Romantic Reformers and the Antislavery Struggle in the Civil War Era*, New York, 2014.)

Embedded within Romanticism were not old-fashioned Whig-republican-federalist notions of liberty and government, but expansive allegiance to French liberté, eqalité, and fraternity, especially as formulated in the second and more radical French Revolution of 1792-1794. Associated with the Jacobins, including Robespierre, the political-philosophical ideas of Jean Jacques Rousseau were popularized and implemented. Spread into Europe by invading armies of the first French Republic, French philosophy and politics took root in their liberal and radical forms (reflecting the differences between the first and moderate French Revolution of 1789-1791 and the second one of 1792-1794).

Under Napoleon between 1803 and 1815 this process was repeated with more French armies marching across Europe and into Russia. After Napoleon's final defeat in 1815, French ideas found willing converts in countries with restored conservative, monarchial, and absolutist regimes. Wars of independence erupted prominently in South America, but also in Greece, Spain, Naples, and Russia. For the wars of independence in Europe after 1815, see Richard Stites, *The Four Horsemen: Riding to Liberty in Post-Napoleonic Europe* (Oxford, UK and New York 2014). These revolutionary movements were "acting on liberal notions" drawn "from the Enlightenment through the French Revolution and from French and English contemporaries."(11-12) Pertinently, the American Revolution was rejected by French revolutionaries. "The French Revolution put an end to the 'American Dream' in French opinion . . . . The reason is that from 1789 on, the French had their own dream . . . ." (François Furet, *In the Workshop of History*, 1984, 160.)

The Napoleonic era and wars of independence and liberation inspired English Romantic writers like Wordsworth and Lord Byron. The latter became very popular in the North and had a great impact upon one William Lloyd Garrison. Liberty as equality and democracy, however, were not American ideas but very much French ones. So, too, was abolition, with the first French Republic leading the way in 1794. (See W. Caleb McDaniel, *The Problem of Democracy in the Age of Slavery: Garrisonian Abolitionists and Transatlantic Reform*, Baton Rouge, 2013.)

This crucial distinction between Anglo and Gallic liberty informed Vernon L. Parrington's *The Romantic Revolution in America, 1800-1860* (New York, 1927). Merrill D. Peterson also noted the difference between English and French liberty in *The Jefferson Image in the American Mind* (New York, 1960). Summarizing the conflicting eulogies of Thomas Jefferson at his death in 1826, Peterson observes that "Liberty was the quintessence, but liberty in what sense?" With Jefferson in mind, "two contrasting, some may say contradictory types of political liberty" were exposed. "One derived from the English legal heritage: the Whggish liberty of individual rights. The other partook of . . . French revolutionary ideology: the democratic liberty of popular rule." (Although Peterson associated the American Revolution with the latter, it was more clearly in the English Whig libertarian tradition, as studies by Bernard Bailyn, Gordon S. Wood, and others demonstrated between 1965 and 1969.)

Of interest here is Peterson's reference to Francis Lieber's formulation of Anglo versus Gallican conceptions of liberty. "The former, he said, was federal and practical, liberty consisting in an intricate system of laws and guarantees. The latter represented 'the idea of equality founded upon or acting through universal suffrage, or . . . the undivided sovereignty of the people with an uncompromising centralism.'" (Peterson, 9-10, 42-43, and 210-211.) Lieber, a German revolutionary, was an important law professor at Columbia at the outbreak of the war in 1861 and a key advisor to Lincoln on the laws of war. Lieber's view of French liberty accurately describes Lincoln's own reinterpretation of American government as being "of the people" and as embodying Rousseau's notion of the national "General Will." Not "the last best hope of earth" but more the beginning of a new birth of freedom with national unification. The "New Nation" promised much but delivered more to the Republican Party than to freedmen, white Southerners, or American Indians during and after America's Civil War.

In *The Union War*, Gary W. Gallagher directly links the new idea of Union as the "nation" to the Romantic movement in the North. "Citizens in the northern states believed the idea of American nationalism was bound up with the ideals of human betterment." The Union as the "nation" was "not a mere political arrangement but the only way an American [in the North] could summarize his romantic concept of national existence." (*The Union War*, 47) The "Slave Power Conspiracy" propaganda of the 1850's made the South inimical to "the nation." The South was retrogressive and threatening, allegedly a nest of oligarchy, inequality, unfree labor, illiteracy, and economic backwardness.

The significance of the "Slave Power Conspiracy" myth, according to Susan-Mary Grant, was manifold: For "many northerners, the idea of such a conspiracy seemed less a threat than a convenient rallying cry against the nation's ills." It provided a means by which many of the contradictions inherent in nineteenth-century American society could, theoretically, be resolved. More particularly,

> The notion of the slave power conspiracy enabled northerners to bridge the gap between the ideals expressed in the Declaration of Independence and the reality of slavery in the nation by sectionalizing the dominant moral dilemma of the age. In sum, the image of the southern slave power conspiracy provided Whig-Republicans with a powerful and persuasive symbol of aristocratic tyranny against

which to define their own political and social vision....
[It strengthened] their arguments in favor of northern
superiority, [and] ultimately reinforced their belief
that northern ideals should, and in time, would,
become national ones. (*North Over South*, 5. See also
David M. Potter, *The Impending Crisis: America Before
the Civil War, 1848-1861*, 1976, and Marc Egnal, *Clash of
Extremes: The Economic Origins of the Civil War*, 2009.)

Even with the failure of immediate abolitionism by 1844,
America was rapidly becoming divided, but not by slavery alone,
for or against. A more accurate description would be a three-way
division between the South, a rapidly developing Romantic North
in the Northeast and Great Lakes region, and the older other
North still sharing the Southern commitment to the ideas and
ideals of the founders of 1776 and framers of 1787-1788. To the
new nation, "human bondage seemed incompatible with the
founding ideals of the republic." To a majority, North and South,
there was no paradox between republican liberty and slavery. The
American republic could co-exist as half-free and half-slave
pending slavery's still hoped for gradual abolition by peaceful
means. (See Potter, *The Impending Crisis* and Marc Egnal, *Clash of
Extremes*.)

## SECESSION—IN DEFENSE OF THE REPUBLIC

With the demise of radical abolitionism in the 1840's, anti-slavery assumed political form in the Liberty and Free Soil parties of 1840-1848. Into the context of an America co-existing half-free and half-slave, slavery's restriction from the new territories was inserted by the anti-slavery North. With yet another Compromise in 1850, the issue of slavery in the territories seemed to be settled. Then came the fateful passage of the Kansas-Nebraska Acts of 1854. A new Republican Party emerged, dedicated to a new principle of "antislavery nationalism" or total prohibition of slavery from the territories by unilateral national authority.

Unlike the old Southern dominance of 1820-1850, the alleged new "Slave Power Conspiracy" had the intention of making slavery a national institution. Exaggerated as this was on the part of Republicans, it proved useful in demanding a national solution to the issue of slavery in the territories (destined to be free soil). It purportedly was a new aggression of slavery that had been denied at the founding and regarded as cause for disunion thereafter. Within a decade after 1850, America was engaged in a civil war. Its cause would not be Southern secession but its denial on the part of Lincoln and the new Republican Party. (See Graham A. Peck, "Abraham Lincoln and the Triumph of Antislavery Nationalism," *Journal of the Abraham Lincoln Association,* 28 [Summer 2007], 1-27.)

At this point, Romantic social-cultural perfectionism was supplanted by the imperative of nineteenth century Romantic nationalism. America's final perfection required the creation of a new nation unified politically and culturally (in the image of the perfectionist-progressive North). Only a homogenous people could form a nation, meaning that diversity and dissent were unacceptable because they were impediments to unity. Every people had a unique genius or *zeitgeist*. This was best expressed in having a state of their own. In practical terms, and before the abolition of slavery, the problem of the "Slave Power" had to be confronted and eliminated. This domination of the federal government by the slaveowners and allied interests in the North had to cease for continued progress to occur. Of course, freed African-Americans were a major contradiction to the imperative of homogeneity but little thought was given to that.

Besides consistently opposing economic policies proposed by Republicans, the "Slave Power" also rejected expansive government in general by insisting on a strict construction of the Constitution. As scoffers of the equal rights of all men its proponents supposedly threatened free white labor in the North with their aristocratic political power. Their adherence to a presumably newly-invented states' rights philosophy (foreign to original national intentions as many were beginning to believe), encouraged "Disunion" by nullification and secession. Allegedly Invented after the Constitution of 1787, states' rights was a shield to protect slavery and preserve the South as an aristocracy by the subjugation of blacks by slavery and plain folk by rule of the few. This imagined danger was an easy sell to the fourth of the Northern population that was now foreign-born.

Not until the rise of the Republican Party of 1854-1856 did Romantic perfectionist reformers and nationalists unite. Not until the election of Lincoln as sixteenth President did minority political, philosophical, and historical views gain control of the presidency and the House of Representatives. United on a platform that promised the total prohibition of slavery from the territories by Congressional authority alone, Lincoln and the Republicans not only moved beyond championing slavery's restriction and repudiation of the old Missouri line of 36° 30'. In doing so they signaled their rejection of the Constitution of 1787-1788 and the end of the American republic as a federal polity that left to states alone final authority over slavery. Most important, as emphasized by Lincoln, America had to cease being half-free and half-slave as it had always been. It had to become all one or the other.

With the Declaration of Independence reinterpreted to be more about equality than a right of revolution, it was now made superior to the Constitution as the first charter of a national government. Indeed, Lincoln claimed that the union was older than the states that it was made up of! To Daniel T. Rodgers, however, the notion of "the Declaration" being "superior to the Constitution, to be sure, was a historical fiction." It was also "a legally impotent document." (*Contested Truths*, 76)

Here, then, was justification for Southern secession. Since Lincoln and Republicans no longer believed in the old union of the states, how could their professions of not interfering with slavery where it existed constitutionally be believed? With political power in the federal government soon to pass to the party of anti-slavery, what assurances would the South have if the Constitution was no longer respected? Recognizing that the newer territories were destined to become free soil by the inexorable demographics of Northern population increase and Northern settlement of the west by those with antislavery and Negrophobic convictions, the South's opposition both to "popular sovereignty" (allowing a mere territorial legislature to decide the issue of slavery) and total prohibition was indeed a matter of constitutional scruple.

For any minority interest in the Union, let alone one where slavery remained important economically and socially, a centralized authority posed a threat to its existence. At the same time, Lincoln and the Republican Party favored economic measures that affected the South adversely. For the South, a separate existence out of a distorted union was the only alternative left beyond submission. Their own political heritage from 1776 and 1787 told them that such submission to hostile authority was to become political slaves of an overbearing and intolerant North, governing by different intentions than those of the founders and framers. In Southern eyes, the North in 1861 had become the imperious British of old, resistance to which had justified American independence.

By refusing a token compromise on the issue of slavery, the Republican Party and Lincoln were actually encouraging Southern secession, knowing full well what the Southern response would be when the thoroughly sectional Republican Party gained control of the government. When Lincoln was elected to the presidency in 1860, what might be became a reality. The South, one state at a time but with internal communications among each amounting to cooperation, proceeded to secede by invoking the right of revolution proclaimed as the primary purpose of the Declaration of 1776 and the sovereign power of the people of the states. To historian Anne Norton, "Southern secessionist sentiment was thus not properly reaction, but reenactment." (*Alternative Americas: A Reading of Antebellum Political Culture*, 1986, 182. See also William J. Cooper, Jr. *We Have the War Upon Us: The Onset of the Civil War, November 1860-April 1861*, New York, 2012.)

Secession was not the cause of America's Civil War. The denial of secession as a legitimate right by Abraham Lincoln and the Republicans was. Lincoln ignored the actions of the people of the states, characterizing them as merely a mob opposing his authority. All else needed was the opportunity to make sure that the Confederates fired the first shot, which result Lincoln assured with his Ft. Sumter relief expedition. After the Confederate bombardment on April 12, Lincoln called for 75,000 volunteers to suppress the "rebellion" down South. Four more Southern states joined the new CSA and the Border States were thrown into civil war. If the "conditional unionism" of many Southerners made them reluctant secessionists, Lincoln's policy of "coercion" was truly a violation of the federal compact. Government by force was tyranny. It was so in 1776 and was so again in 1861! So said President Buchanan and his Attorney General and many other Northerners. (See Russell McClintock, *Lincoln and the Decision for War: The Northern Response to*

*Secession*, 2008, and Daniel W. Crofts, *Reluctant Confederates: Upper South Unionists in the Secession Crisis*, 1993.)

The issue that led to a civil war in 1861-1865 was not anti-slavery as abolition and certainly not black equality. It was keeping blacks, and white Southerners too, out of future states. It was, above all, about the Constitution and the nature of the union and political power. Shaping "the operation of sectionalism was the prevailing concept of the negative state and strong limitations on the power of the central government. These limitations meant, in effect, that Congress could do little about slavery except to talk about it." "Southerners had insisted repeatedly that they did not expect slavery to go into the Southwest but they objected to having Congress make an invidious distinction between their institutions and those of the North." "With apprehensions such as these [increasing free soil political power and continuing threats of abolition], many southerners had come to believe that they faced a crucial choice: they must somehow stabilize their position in the Union with safeguards to preserve the security of the slave system before the minority position made them impotent." (Potter, *The Impending Crisis*, 29, 91, 94.)

Southerners were right after all. They were not the "revolutionists"; Lincoln and the Republicans, and the abolitionists before them were. Quoting Richard Taylor in 1865, about what a "turning point" the Civil War was, the Louisiana planter and Confederate general knew what he was saying in light of America's and the world's history between 1776 and 1865. "The [French] revolution of '89 did not produce a greater change in the 'Ancien Régime' than this has in our social life." (*Battle Cry of Freedom*, 861)

It is not be too far-fetched to suggest that the Northern-Romantic-Perfectionist-Nationalist origins of our Civil War can be traced back to the French Revolutions of 1789-99 and its long impact on the Atlantic world extending into the 19th century. Such is the claim made here once the connections between Jacobinism, radicalism, egalitarianism, abolitionism, nationalism, and Romanticism are made and understood. Many years ago, in *The Romantic Revolution in America, 1800-1860* (1927), volume two of *Main Currents in American Thought*, Vernon L. Parrington was ahead of his time when he declared that "It is the North that has changed and not the South, and the nationality that sits so easily upon us would have seemed ominous to the simpler world that determined the ideals of the Old Dominion [and Jefferson, Madison, and others of the founding generation]." (3)

## THE NATIONALIST MYTH

A year into the American Civil War of Northern-Romantic-Perfectionist-Nationalist origins, after the denial of secession as a legitimate right of revolution and of the true nature of the Union, "the nation" trumped all other considerations, political and historical. Lincoln made these telling remarks in 1862: "The dogmas of the quiet past are inadequate to the stormy present. The occasion is piled high with difficulty and we must rise with the occasion. As our case is new, so we must think anew, and act anew. We must disenthrall ourselves, and then we shall save our country." (www.civil-war-enthusiast.com/abraham-lincoln) Lincoln and abolitionists were "badly in need of tools with which to hack away at the protective coil of ordinary law wound around slavery." The "transcendent status of the Declaration" thus became "an indispensable point of faith." (*Contested Truths*, 76)

Historical myth-making was used by Lincoln and Republicans to persuade voters in key states to support a new "Republican" party that had nothing to do with the first one of James Madison and Thomas Jefferson in the 1790's. By a myth of Democracy, as it is termed here, Lincoln and Republicans had reinterpreted the principles of 1776 and 1787 by imparting to the founders beliefs they did not espouse. This substitute inheritance was of nineteenth century origin and not even American. Comprising much different intentions beyond original Whig-republican ones, these newer "isms" were rightfully characterized as radical and even "fanatical."

Mary-Susan Grant, in *North Over South*, has well described nationalism's progress in America before the Civil War and the role of the Republican Party in appropriating it for partisan purposes, including justification for unification by force. "The Republican Party in the 1850's was engaged in, and was partly the result of, a process of national construction by which the American national ideal became associated with the North in general and the Republican Party in particular." "At its core [Northern Republican ideology] was the belief that the South was a world apart from the North, and that the differences between them did not derive from slavery alone." "Convinced that their democracy was superior, northerners could no more allow the secession of the southern states in 1861 than they could permit the South to remain in the Union unchanged." (*North Over South*, 2000, 8-9)

The Republican ascendancy in 1860 over the Democrats reflected a large country truly divided by real differences — politically, socially, economically, culturally, and in historical understanding. Beyond slavery for or against, Americans were different peoples with conflicting and irreconcilable beliefs. "I fear Northerner and Southerner are aliens, not merely in social and political arrangements, but in mental and moral constitution." So wrote Philadelphia Republican George Templeton Strong in December of 1860. (Quoted in *North Over South* before the Introduction.)

Again James M. McPherson provides expert commentary about the many issues beyond slavery dividing the North and the South in 1860:

> Thus when secessionists protested that they were acting to preserve traditional rights and values, they were correct. They fought to protect their constitutional liberties against the perceived northern threat to overthrow them. The South's concept of republicanism had not changed in three-quarters of a century; the North's had. With complete sincerity the South fought to preserve its version of the republic of the founding fathers—a government of limited powers that protected the rights of property and whose constituency comprised an independent gentry and yeomanry of the white race undisturbed by large cities, heartless factories, restless free workers, and class conflict.

At the same time:

> The accession to power of the Republican party, with
> its ideology of competitive, egalitarian, free labor
> capitalism, was a signal to the South that the northern
> majority had turned irrevocably toward this
> frightening, revolutionary future. Indeed, the Black
> Republican party appeared to the eyes of many
> southerners as "essentially a revolutionary party"
> composed of "a motley throng of Sans culottes . . .
> Infidels and freelovers, interspersed by Bloomer
> women, fugitive slaves, and amalgamationists."
> Therefore secession was a pre-emptive
> counterrevolution to prevent the Black Republican
> revolution from engulfing the South.

In the same book, *Battle Cry of Freedom*, which is regarded as the
highest contemporary authority on the Civil War, Prof. McPherson
further dispels one of the great misinterpretations of the American
past: that of a reactionary South in the antebellum era that turned its
back on the liberal and democratic, egalitarian, democratic, and
nationalist beliefs of the founders of the republic and embraced
instead an invented states' rights philosophy for the sole purpose of
protecting slavery. "From a broader perspective," he observes, "it
may be that the North that was exceptional and unique before the
Civil War."

> The South more closely resembled a majority of the
> societies in the world than did the rapidly changing
> North during the antebellum generation. Despite the
> abolition of legal slavery or serfdom throughout much
> of the western hemisphere and western Europe, most
> of the world . . . like the South had an unfree or quasi-
> free labor force. Most societies in the world remained
> predominantly rural, agricultural, and labor
> intensive.... most like the South remained bound by
> traditional values and networks of family kinship,
> hierarchy, and patriarchy. The North . . . along with a
> few countries of Western Europe . . . hurtled forward

eagerly toward a future of industrial capitalism that many southerners found distasteful if not frightening; the South remained proudly and even defiantly rooted in the past before 1861 . . . . Union victory in the war destroyed the southern vision of America and ensured that the northern vision would become the American vision. Until 1861, however, it was the North that was out of the American mainstream, not the South. Of course, the northern states, along with Britain and a few countries in northwestern Europe, were cutting a new channel in world history that would doubtless have become the mainstream if the American Civil War had not happened. Russia had abolished serfdom in 1861 to complete the dissolution of the ancient institution of bound labor in Europe . . . . (860 ff.)

## BEYOND EMANCIPATION

But why did the abolition of slavery in North America alone require a civil war to achieve? Why was emancipation not proclaimed at the outset rather than later? Why did Lincoln and Republicans not just wait and allow the demographic forces favoring the North to play out and make the territories free-soil with increased political power in their favor and for their interests? Above all, why did abolition not lead to black equality after 1865?

The answer is to be found in Romantic nationalism of the nineteenth century that was the central aim of Lincoln and the Republicans. Abolition was not only limited to the legal end of slavery as the right of ownership of humans as property, and never about black equality, but emancipation before the Thirteenth Amendment was likewise more of a war measure designed to lessen the Confederacy's ability to resist militarily than a humanitarian program. Far from preserving the union of old as Lincoln and the Republicans claimed they were doing, they were really making it anew into a nation, the states united with "U. S." now being rendered in the singular.

Among "other certain large consequences of the war," that "Secession and slavery were killed, never to be revived," there was the new nation. In the transition from "Union" to "nation," Lincoln's "own wartime speeches betokened the transition." On July 4, 1861, in his Special Message to Congress, Lincoln "used 'Union' thirty-two times and 'nation' three times." Writing to Horace Greeley in 1862, "Lincoln spoke of the 'Union' eight times and of the 'nation' not at all." At Gettysburg, Lincoln "did not refer to the 'Union' at all but used the word 'nation' five times to invoke a new birth of freedom and nationalism for the United States." Lincoln in "his second inaugural address . . . spoke of one side seeking to dissolve the *Union* in 1861 and the other accepting the challenge of war to preserve the *nation*." (859)

Having admitted that "Union" and "nation" were not synonymous terms, McPherson, by no means alone, cannot come to the conclusion that it was the North, represented by Lincoln and the Republicans, that changed beliefs and waged war against the South for nationalist purposes above slavery's abolition. Susan-Mary Grant does so in her *North over South: Northern Nationalism and American Identity in the Antebellum Era* (2000). "As a result of the Civil War, the antebellum Union was replaced by an integrated state with both territorial and political sovereignty."

The Civil War offered the North the opportunity to enforce its own particular vision of American nationalism [not present at the creation], by force of arms rather than by force of argument that its vision of America's future was the only viable one.

Although equally keen to align themselves with the ideals of the revolutionary generation, northerners found it difficult to break through this particular part of the South's defenses. As it was understood at the start of the war, the Revolution seemed better suited as justification for the Confederacy than as a prop for the Union. To acknowledge that the South was engaged in an act of revolution was, in a very real sense, to validate secession and to recognize that the South had the right to attempt to establish a Confederate nation. Faced with this deadly combination of emotive and legalistic argument in favor of secession, northerners struggled to offer not just an alternative but an overwhelmingly persuasive argument in support of their assertion that America was constructed as one nation and ought to remain so.

If "the Confederacy was, in reality, less romantic than history has chosen to portray it, then the North was certainly more idealistic than it sometimes appeared . . . . Lincoln knew very well that there was much more at stake in the Federal war effort than the maintenance of the Union." "Yet by resorting to warfare to compel a national identity that was clearly not going to be established by voluntary means, the North found itself in the paradoxical position of breaking the original contract of the Declaration of Independence in the process of defending it. Ultimately, the emancipation of the slaves and the passage of the Thirteenth and Fourteenth Amendments were not accompanied by any obvious lessening of racism."(*North over South*, 2000, 154, 163, 167, 168, 171)

Myth-making, as Professor Marc Ferro reminds us in *The Use and Abuse of History* (London, 1984) is an almost universal phenomenon engaged in by all peoples and societies be it American, African, Asian Indian, Arabic, Islamic, Armenian, or European. Among the reasons cited by Ferro for this long-lived practice are (1) the need to ennoble the past by ignoring more sordid events and developments (as with the origin of the caste system in India); (2) to establish continuity and uniformity in ideology and political rule (as in Communist Russia and among Muslims); (3) to explain away a debilitating past and/or to avoid troublesome issues; (4) to promote nationalism and patriotism; and (5) to justify war and imperialism. This list of causal factors in the myth-making process applies as well to the North during the antebellum period. While studies of American myths abound, their larger political meaning has heretofore escaped notice.

That it was the North doing the myth-making rather than the South not only fits Ferro's model of historical reinterpretation or misinterpretation, it also squares with the historical reality of the "Age of Revolution and Reform" from 1815-60 both in Europe and America. Buffeted by the revolutions of Romanticism and Industrialism after 1815, Europeans experienced their own contest of ideas and struggle for power among competing political and social groups. On one side were the conservatives (monarchs, aristocrats, and capitalists) seeking to maintain the status quo against the liberal and radical demands of democrats, republicans, and socialists. In

Europe, the forces for and against change clashed dramatically in the attempted revolutions of 1848. Scared as hell at the thought of another French Revolution, the conservatives enacted reforms (political, constitutional, and social) from above to prevent revolution from below. The result was not civil war(s), but the responsive conservative state!

If Romantic perfectionism fueled individualism and social reform, the nationalistic element of that revolutionary ideology gave rise to the idea of the state or nation as the best means for the fulfillment of a new society. Expressed by Johann Herder and other German writers, in the wake of the wars of the French Revolution and Napoleon (1792-1815), nationalism in the sense of unifying a people of common culture and language led to the unification of Italy in 1870 and Germany in 1871. In this context, the American Civil War of 1861-65 has a chronological significance not fully appreciated. What happened in America, in short, was part of a larger world pattern of revolution, reform, and unification. But here the radicals [Lincoln and the Republicans] triumphed over the liberals of the founding era and their successors.

## WHY TODAY'S HISTORIANS DON'T AGREE

In conclusion, we come to a most perplexing question: If the South was right all along about the legitimacy of secession and in its historical interpretation of early American history, and if it was the North that changed, why do Americans and most scholars believe otherwise? Suffice it to say for now that American and Southern history were rewritten by Northerners to give us the consensus view that still predominates today. For all of the studies of our Civil War, its most important consequence has yet to be discerned. Not only did it make us a new nation with a new constitution, but it also gave us a new national history or mythology in the form of the twin myths of Democracy (America was born modern, democratic, egalitarian, anti-slavery if not abolitionist, and fully unified as a nation) and a reactionary South (which because of slavery turned its back on the liberal ideas and ideals of the founders, and invented a new states' rights philosophy as the means to protect its "peculiar institution"). The myth of "proslavery as an aberration in American history" is examined in Larry E. Tise, *Proslavery: A History of the Defense of Slavery in America, 1701-1840*, 1987, xiv, xviii, 3-11. Tise *shows conclusively that proslavery ideas were a product more of Northern than of Southern culture.

Essential as this national myth was to justifying a Northern war against the South that was always about more than slavery alone, it also and falsely made slavery the sole cause of civil war in America and as such totally the responsibility of the South. In 21st century America, however, the myths of democracy and a reactionary South still inform writing about the war's causes and consequences. In simple terms, the North was right historically and constitutionally, and the South was wrong. Slavery was the sole cause of the conflict and the central theme of Southern history as well that which ultimately drove it to disunion. Abraham Lincoln and the Republican Party, triumphant in the presidential election of 1860, had no choice but to preserve the Union and abolish slavery to assure the blessings of liberty for all promised by the Declaration of Independence and secured by the Constitution.

Interestingly, McPherson speaks to the Northern origins of a "Great Reaction" below the Mason-Dixon line. While Union soldiers were not engaged in the cause of black freedom before the Emancipation Proclamation of 1863, that motivation did increase thereafter with about 50 percent of the Federals approving Lincoln's controversial action. Equally motivating to Federal soldiers was the cause of democracy against an aristocratic South. In the words of a Minnesota lieutenant, "An Aristocracy brought on this war – that Aristocracy must be broken up ... it is rotten and corrupt .... God intends that it and slavery ... must go down together ...." (*For Cause & Comrades: Why Men Fought in the Civil War*, 1997, 124, 126)

Put another way, not the *republican* South as the defender of original intentions but the *imagined one of aristocracy and slavery* (notwithstanding the fact that most antebellum white Southerners were non-slaveholders and enjoyed representative government) had to be excised from the body politic. It was replaced by the image of the North based upon a reinterpretation of the principles of 1776 and 1787 which made them the true heirs to the framers and founders rather than the South. In the end, the creation of a new history for a new nation was a critical part of the Northern path to war against the South.

Finally, America's Civil War of 1861-65 was inevitable. It had to happen because Romantic Nationalism in the North demanded political unification. The creation of the states united was a first step toward the Reconstruction of America itself. A quotation from the *Boston Post* of May 16, 1861, is most revealing (from *North Over South*, 19, 153).

> Now the truth is that American nationality ... is a thing of ideas solely and not a thing of races. It is neither English nor Irish, nor Dutch, nor French; it is not Puritan or Cavalier; it is not North or South; our nationality is our self-government, our system of popular liberty and equal law .... This is the age of nationalities. Fired by our example, the oppressed of the world have aspired to the dignity of nationalities. Shall the first to set the example, and the grandest in the procession of nations, suffer its nationality to depart, at the bidding not of a foreign foe, but rebel traitors of the soil?

Simultaneously with war against the South, the subjugation of the first Americans, Amerindians, commenced in 1862 and continued until 1890 and the massacre at Wounded Knee. With effective resistance ended, the Indians of the Plains were forced onto reservations to "civilize" them and to make way for more white settlers and free labor that new transcontinental railroads would transport. Literally, these iron rails united a new America. Ironically, again, newly freed male slaves as "Buffalo Soldiers" joined in the killing of other persons of color. At the same time the vast majority of freed black people remained in the South, ineligible for the free land being given away in the West.

More than a conflict between North and South and between liberty and slavery, our Civil War was really a contest between two different Americas. On the one hand, there was the original republic born in the late 18th century and symbolized by the South and the other North. On the other hand, there was the North (or a revolutionary part of it) symbolized by the Republican Party of Lincoln, which embodied newer ideas of government, society, and politics of 19th century origins (particularly Romantic nationalism and perfectionism). With the defeat of the South in 1865, the old republic and federal union of the states were no more. The South's defense of the republic and federalism begun long before 1860 became a "Lost Cause" with the triumph of the North and the myths of Democracy and a Reactionary South. At the same time, republicanism itself and original intentions 18th century style were lost to history for a century at least until their recovery by scholars in the 1960s and 1970s.

Mainstream scholars are reluctant to give credit to the well-supported conclusion that the South was right all along about the Constitution and the Revolution. The "politically correct" history profession have had things their way for too long now. Yet their own version of American and Southern history is itself based on the first P.C. campaign in our republic's history, the one waged by the North against the South in the years before our Civil War. Then was invented a new American history that made democracy, egalitarianism, nationalism, and abolition into our national ideals. The positions of the North and South were reversed. America became the reinterpreted principles of 1776 and 1787 and the republicanism of the South became perverted into an anti-democratic defense of aristocracy and then of slavery. The myth of a reactionary (and illiberal and un-American) South was born as the necessary corollary of the myth of Democracy. To quote Michael Kammen, "Continuity (combined with consistency) epitomizes the dominant view held by most Americans even remotely interested in these issues during the last two centuries." (*Sovereignty and Liberty: Constitutional Discourse in American Culture* [Madison, 1988], 45.

Modifying this stereotyping of the South by abolitionists and Republicans was what the "Revisionist" historians of the 1920s through 1950s were all about. It makes them relevant again to the Northern origins of America's Civil War. See Avery O. Craven, *The Coming of the Civil War*, 1942, 1957; Howard Floan, *The South in Northern Eyes, 1831-1861*, 1956; and Michael E. Woods, *Emotional and Sectional Conflict in the Antebellum United States,* 2014. War against the South was always about more than slavery alone, and the Lost Cause of the South is heavily documented and historically sound. Since the Civil War on both sides was really about 1776 and 1787, and what the founders and framers believed or not, it is essential to distinguish reality from myth. Thus, the need to begin with radical Whig-republican ideology and to define this most important set of beliefs and to trace its persistence in the South through the Civil War era. With this political-constitutional-historical foundation, the North's deviation from the true founding in the 19th century becomes manifest. We must look anew at the central theme of Southern history and the origins of the Civil War as the prerequisite foundations for an alternative history of America from the Revolution to the conflict of 1861-1865 and beyond.

\* \* \*

"America's Romantic Age had produced a Civil War." (David Goldfield, *America Aflame: How the Civil War Created a Nation* [New York: Bloomsbury Press, 2012], 13.)

\* \* \*

"The legacy of the Civil War in Victorian America, according to Rose, was the triumph of kind of humanistic romanticism." (Mitchell G. Klingenberg, Texas Christian University, review of Anne C. Rose, *Victorian America and the Civil War* [Cambridge, UK and New York: Cambridge University Press, 1992], at

http://personal.tcu.edu/woodworth/Rose-VAATC.htm.)

\* \* \*

"Living in an age of romantic nationalism nowhere more intense than in the United States, Lincoln had become a devotee of the cult of the Union as preached by Webster and Clay." (David M. Potter, *The Impending Crisis: America Before the Civil War, 1848-1861* [New York and London: HarperCollins, 1976, HarperPerennial, 2011], 343.)

\* \* \*

"Romanticism was conceived from political philosophy expressed in manifestoes and journalism, sometimes written by imaginative writers and sometimes influencing them." (R.S. White, *Natural Rights and the Birth of Romanticism in the 1790s* [New York and London: Palgrave MacMillan, 2005], 3.)

\* \* \*

"It was meaningless to the historian [to ask 'if the natural rights philosophy of the Declaration of Independence is true or false ...'] since it had no bearing on the actual purpose of the Declaration: the justification of American independence to the world." (Merrill D. Peterson, *The Jefferson Image in the American Mind* [Oxford, UK, and New York: Oxford University Press, 1960, 1962], 308.)

* * *

"Fed by German metaphysics, as well as the Marshall-Story-Webster stream of constitutional theory, the movement to establish a unitary national theory of sovereignty claimed the energies of American political scientists for forty years to come. Jefferson held almost no status with these scholars, not only because his theory of federal relations was antagonistic to the theory of 'national existence,' but also because his theory of the relations of rulers to the ruled did not permit the requisite degree of organic unity, allegiance, and permanence in the polity. Numerous popular histories of the Civil War from Northern pens expressed similar ideas in vulgar terms. The image of the 'great heretic' or 'great conspirator' was prominent in their pages." (Peterson, *The Jefferson Image in the American Mind*, 220.)

* * *

"The first gun fired at Fort Sumter, smashed the old Union and with it the political design of Thomas Jefferson. The War seemed suddenly to have rendered the fabled age of the republic unusable." (Peterson, *ibid.*, 216.)

* * *

"State rights might be humbug in fact, but it was a very convenient theory. The people were sovereign, not collectively as 'one people,' but separately as several states; therefore, they could by the exercise of their sovereignty in state conventions secede from the Union. South Carolina scrupulously observed the theory in December 1860. Others took considerable liberties with it. Generally, however, the secession movement was a remarkable testament to the compact theory of government, which Jefferson more than anyone, had fixed upon the American political mind." (Peterson, *ibid.*, 213.)

* * *

"Liberty was the quintessence; but liberty in what sense? If the eulogies [of 1826] are read with an eye for their theoretical purport, they associated Jefferson with two contrasting, some may say contradictory, types of political liberty. One derived from English legal heritage, the Whiggish liberty of individual rights. The other partook strongly of American and French revolutionary ideology: the democratic liberty of popular rule. Was Jefferson the conservative guardian of the law or the flaming prophet of democracy? The eulogists gave no clear-cut answer to the question, the irresoluble ambiguity, in the American polity. He embodied the ambiguity. Repeatedly in his posthumous history he was to be caught up in the dilemma of a nation committed both to a system of constituted rights and to the sovereignty of the people." (Peterson, *ibid.*, 10.)

\* \* \*

"The final statement was [Thomas] Hutchinson's, and it was prophetic. You believe, he said in his recapitulation, that 'a *subordinate* power in government ..., whilst it keeps within its limits [*imperium in imperio*], is not subject to the control of the *supreme power*. This is illogical, for how can there be 'a *subordinate* power without a power superior to it? Must it not, so far as it is without control, be itself supreme?" "It is essential to the being of government that a power should always exist which no other power within such government can have right to withstand and control. Therefore, when the word *power* relates to the supreme power of government it must be understood *absolute and unlimited.*'"(Bernard Bailyn, *The Ideological Origins of the American Revolution* [Cambridge, Massachusetts: Harvard University Press, 1967], 222.)

\* \* \*

"Leading Americans like John Dickinson continued to insist – though now with increasing desperation – that 'the sovereignty over the colonies must be limited,' that 'a line there must be,' in principle as well as in fact, setting off Parliament's powers from those of the colonial legislatures, and that this line gave to the English government control of the commerce and foreign affairs of the colonies and to the colonial Assemblies 'exclusive right of internal legislation,' including taxing." (Bailyn, *ibid.*, 223.)

* * *

"The belief that 'imperium in imperio' was a solecism and the assumption that 'sovereignty of the people' and the sovereignty of an organ of government were of the same order of things would remain to haunt the efforts of those who would struggle to build a stable system of federal government. But the initial challenges to the traditional 18th-century notion of sovereignty had been made. Later analysts, starting where the colonists had left off before Independence and habituated to think in terms of 'qualified sovereignty,' 'lesser sovereignty,' 'the divisibility of sovereignty,' would continue the effort to make federalism a logical as well as a practical system of government .... But the federal tradition, born in the colonists' efforts to state in constitutional language the qualification of Parliament's authority they had known ... nevertheless arrived, and remains, to justify the distribution of absolute power among governments no one of which can claim to be total, and so to keep the central government from amassing 'a degree of energy, in order to sustain itself, dangerous to the liberties of the people..'" (Bailyn, *ibid.*, 229.)

* * *

"Republican government 'may do well enough for a single city or small territory, but would be utterly improper for such a continent as this. America is too unwieldy for the feeble, dilatory, administration of democracy.' 'Democracy,' that was the point. 'Republic' and 'democracy' were words closely associated in the colonists' minds; often they were used synonymously; and they evoked a mixed response of enthusiasm and foreboding. For if 'republic' conjured up for many the positive features of the Commonwealth era and marked the triumph of virtue and reason, 'democracy,' a word that denoted the lowest order of society as well as the form of government in which the commons ruled, was generally associated with the threat of civil disorder and the early assumption of power by a dictator. Throughout the colonial period, and increasingly in the early Revolutionary years, the dangers of 'democratical despotism' preyed on the minds not merely of crown officials and other defenders of prerogative but all of enlightened thinkers." (Bailyn, *ibid.*, 282-283.)

* * *

"The leaders of the Revolutionary movement were radicals—but they were 18th-century radicals concerned, like the 18th-century English radicals, not with the need to recast the social order nor with the problems of economic inequality and the injustices of stratified societies but with the need to purify a corrupt [British] constitution and fight off the apparent growth of prerogative power." (Bailyn, *ibid.*, 283.)

* * *

"They [Southern thinkers] examined Scripture; their Bible argument is really something more than an exercise in equivocation; it is a strong historical exegesis, and on this plane the Southern divines had clearly the better of their Northern counterparts." (Eric L. McKitrick, ed, *Slavery Defended: The Views of the Old South*. Englewood Cliffs, New Jersey: Prentice-Hall, Incorporated, 1963], 2.)

* * *

# II. "Republicanism" is the Key

IN 1978, THE AUTHOR COMPLETED his Ph.D. at the University of South Carolina. The title of the dissertation was "The Union of the States: A Study of Radical Whig-Republican Ideology and its Influence upon the Nation and the South, 1776-1861." Several ideas were advanced:

- The central theme of Southern history was not slavery, race, or romanticism but republicanism.
- The South (along with the Old North) remained true to and consistent with the principles of 1776 and 1787.
- The North (or a revolutionary part of it) reinterpreted the Founding in the 19th century.
- The Lost Cause of the South and the Confederacy was an historically legitimate case that needed to be re-examined as such.
- The Declaration of 1776 was about independence more than equality.
- The Constitution of 1787-88 was no mystical founding of a "nation" but only a plan of government to be accepted (with amendments) or rejected.
- The Constitution established a confederate republic of a compound nature as described by Alexander Hamilton in *The Federalist* No. 9.
- The view of the essential meaning of 1776 and 1787 maintained by the South before, during, and after the War between the States was correct, contrary to Lincoln and most historians since.

The basis for my conclusions was the emergence of an historical literature of "republicanism" in the late 1960s and early 1970s and with it the recovery of our original beliefs as a people. This scholarship involved an exploration of the intellectual world and motives of the American Founding generation of unprecedented depth and with a trans-Atlantic perspective. The most noted "mainstream" works of this school were H. Trevor Colbourn's *The Lamp of Experience: Whig History and the Intellectual Origins of the American Revolution* (1965); Bernard Bailyn's *The Ideological Origins of the American Revolution*; and Gordon S. Wood's *The Coming of the American Revolution, 1776 – 1787*, although many less celebrated scholars also contributed to it.

I argued that Southern beliefs in states' rights, strict construction, agrarianism, federalism, secession (really the right of revolution contained in the Declaration of Independence), and the South's continued opposition to majoritarianism, capitalism, industrialism, and urbanism were all consistent with the radical Whig-republican ideology that had informed the founders of the American republic in the late 18th century. Here was proof that the ideas of Lincoln and the Republican party were in fact the new "isms" of the day.

Transformative as the Industrial Revolution was, even more disruptive was the "Romantic Revolution of 1800-60" which inspired perfectionism and many reform movements leading to radical abolitionism (far beyond antislavery). When immediate abolition failed in the 1840s, forcible unification or nationalism as the final and imperative "ism" came to the forefront as the means to the goal of an America without slavery. Only by conquering the South could "a new birth of freedom" be assured. Extinction of the South would rid the "nation" of a region that denied the alleged egalitarianism of 1776 and was the source of "disunion" that inevitably flowed from the perverse theory of states' rights. The emancipation of slaves first required emancipation from the South and from "original intentions."

It was the North that had changed and not the South, and therein is to be found the real Northern-Romantic-perfectionism-nationalist origins of the Civil War. Nineteenth century egalitarianism, nationalism, and abolitionism were not expressions of the ideals of 1776 and 1787 as Americans have long believed. They were in fact newer ideas imported from German-speaking Europe through New England and gradually exported to the larger North. Born of the second and radical French Revolution of 1792-94 that culminated in a Reign of Terror, Jacobin ideas of liberté, égalité, and fraternité became goals to be realized by state power.

From the wars of the French Republic and Napoleon, 1792-1815, German romantic nationalism was born in response to foreign invasion and occupation. Multi-faceted as it was—with liberal, conservative, and radical wings—this philosophy is the chief concern here along with its many revolutionary implications for government, society, and politics in the 19th century in Europe and the Americas, North and South.

Advocates of radical French ideas of liberty, equality, democracy, abolitionism, nationalism, and socialism were identified collectively with the pejorative term of "Jacobin" from 1792 through the American Civil War. This is seen, for example, in the writings of Edmund Burke and other early critics of the French Revolution, the Federalist opponents of Jeffersonian republicans in the 1790s, and anti-abolitionists and non-Republicans, North and South, in the years between 1830 and 1860. The fanaticism of these "Jacobins" in Europe and in America was not exaggerated by any means if the term "fanatic" is properly understood in regard to John Brown and his many aiders and abettors— Ralph Waldo Emerson, Henry David Thoreau, and other New England saints.

In America, Romantic perfectionism begot in the North a new Republican Party of 1854-60. The party's rallying cry of "Free Soil, Free Labor, and Free Men" invoked national authority unilaterally to prohibit slavery totally from the territories. Lincoln and

Republicans were firmly opposed to any black people in the territories, slave or free. Their contradiction between racism and non-extension of slavery was more about provoking Southern secession (that they could then reject in the name of the union as absolute) than an embrace of black equality. So much for Lincoln-Republican racial egalitarianism! In Romantic terms, nationalism took precedence over perfectionism, as abolition was limited to freedom from legal slavery only. When emancipation occurred finally and fully in 1865, the Republicans made sure that America's experiment in biracial politics took place on Southern rather than Northern soil!

Romanticism has been said to characterize the Old South. Romanticism in the South and secession as "nationalism" was given classic if mythical expression in Rollin G. Osterweis, *Romanticism and Nationalism in the Old South* (New Haven, 1949). Osterweis would later publish *The Myth of the Lost Cause, 1865-1900* (Hamden, Connecticut, 1973). But philosophically speaking, secession had nothing to do with "the romantic nationalism" of the 19th century, although such Southern nationalism began to develop with the hardships of hostile invasion. It was no more than a right of self-government, derived from the Declaration of Independence of 1776 and the sovereignty of the people of the states. In 1860-61, the South versus the North was a reprise of the colonial-imperial impasse between British empire and colonial self-government that led to American independence. Just as the colonies advocated local rights within the historical context of a limited monarchy and shared power, so too did the South assert the rights of states versus unlimited American government. Just as George III denied *imperium in imperio* in favor of absolute government, refused to compromise, and said that "blows must decide the contest," so too did the Republican Party once it had control of the central government. Rejecting any compromise related to slavery, including extension of the Missouri Compromise line of 36°30′ to the Pacific, Lincoln and the Republicans further denied the right of revolution. War commenced on April 15, 1861, with Lincoln's call for 75,000 volunteers to suppress the "rebellion" down South.

## THE PRINCIPLES OF 1776 AND 1787

Well, my proposed historiographical revolution failed. No rewriting of the past occurred as a result of my efforts to put the South and the Civil War into a new perspective (both American and internationally). Old views continued to be reiterated *ad nauseam* and erroneously; to wit, the South was solely responsible for the Civil War, which was about the single issue of slavery — which had caused the South after 1830 to invent newer ideas of government, society, and politics to protect its "peculiar institution." So, the South and the Confederacy continued to be viewed as reactionary elements of American history and thus out of the mainstream. There were no lessons here to be learned except that slavery and rebellion were wrong and the South paid the price for its sins.

Yet perseverance has its rewards and it is indeed pleasing to be confirmed in many of my essential viewpoints. Not only is republicanism and its many historical implications still an area of ongoing research (albeit a declining one), its applicability to the Civil War has received a more recent and authoritative affirmation. I refer here, of course, to the works of James M. McPherson who is recognized as one of the foremost experts on the Civil War era. Besides *Battle Cry of Freedom: The Civil War Era* (New York: Oxford University Press, 1988), already quoted at length above, McPherson has published *What They Fought For, 1861-1865* (Baton Rouge: LSU, 1994) and *For Cause & Comrades: Why Men Fought in the Civil War* (New York: Oxford University Press, 1997).

*For Cause & Comrades* is the most exhaustive analysis yet of Civil War soldiers' ideas and motivations. McPherson's "findings and interpretations ... rest on reading of letters and diaries in 574 manuscript collections in 22 research libraries and in private possession, plus diaries or sets of letters that were edited and published in 214 books and 403 periodical articles ...." Altogether, some "25,000 to 30,000 letters helped build up the composite portrait of Civil War soldiers" presented in *For Cause & Comrades.* (183) The origins of this particular book go back to a visit undertaken by McPherson with a history class to the Gettysburg battlefield in 1976. Remembering Pickett's charge of 13,000 Confederate soldiers "under artillery and then rifle fire almost every step of the way," the question arose as to why. "What made these men do it?" While defense of home, family and personal honor and religion all played parts in men's motivation on both sides, chapter 8 on "The Cause of Liberty" is most instructive because it is the most obscured aspect of the Confederate cause. To quote McPherson, "The profound irony of the Civil War was that, like Davis and Lincoln, Confederate and Union soldiers interpreted the heritage of 1776 in opposite ways. Confederates professed to fight for liberty and independence from a tyrannical government ...." (3, 104)

"The rhetoric of liberty that had permeated the letters of Confederate volunteers in 1861 grew even stronger as the war progressed. A corporal in the 9th Alabama celebrated his 20th birthday in 1862 by proudly writing in his diary that 'I am engaged in the glorious cause of liberty and justice, fighting for all that we of the South hold dear.'" "The lieutenant colonel of the 10th Tennessee declared in May 1862 that 'my whole heart is in the cause of the Confederacy, because I believe that the perpetuity of Republican principles on this Continent depends upon our success.'" "From the diary of a Missouri Confederate, the words 'fighting gloriously for the undying principles of Constitutional liberty and self government' are to be found. In 1863, a

Confederate officer wrote the following to his wife: 'I am sick of war [and] the separation from the dearest objects of life.' Yet, 'were the contest again just commenced I would willingly undergo it again for the sake of ... our country's independence and liberty.'" (105, 106, 13)

While the defense of slavery was avowed by some Confederates, "most Southern volunteers believed they were fighting for liberty as well as slavery." "Southern recruits waxed most eloquent about their intention to fight against slavery than for it ... that is, against their own [political] enslavement by the North." As one South Carolinian put it, "Sooner than submit to Northern slavery, I prefer death." "If we should suffer ourselves to be subjugated by the tyrannical government of the North, our property will be confuscated [sic] ... & our people reduced to the most abject bondage & utter degradation." Thus, this Virginia private continued, "every Southern heart [must] respond to the language of the great Patrick Henry in the days of '76 & say give me Liberty or give me death."

In quantifying Southern opinion on the Civil War, McPherson concludes as follows: "It would be wrong, however, to assume that Confederate soldiers were constantly preoccupied with this matter [slavery]. In fact, only 20 percent of the sample of 429 soldiers explicitly voiced proslavery convictions in their letters or diaries." (Moreover, "Patriotic and ideological convictions were an essential part of the sustaining motivation of Civil War soldiers." (19-21, 110, 114)

Another other point deserves mention here. There is an accumulating literature which pictures the Confederacy as riven by class antagonism and as unsupported by the non-slaveholding population. Writes McPherson of soldiers' letters: "There is less emphasis on these [class] tensions than in recent scholarship." While anti-Confederate sentiment was expressed, McPherson notes, "The soldiers who felt this way furnished a disproportionate number of deserters and skulkers ... according to the letters of highly motivated volunteers." Current literature overstates social tensions and disaffection within the Confederacy. McPherson writes: "Research in the letters and diaries of Civil War soldiers will soon lead the attentive historian to a contrary conclusion. Ideological motifs almost leap from many pages of these documents."

The "emergence of an understanding of republicanism" or rather "the untold history of an idea" is only one part of a much larger revisionist view of American and Southern history. There's also world history to be considered in relation to its impact upon the course of American development between the War for American Independence and the War Between the States.

The more World History is studied the more one appreciate how events in Europe in particular impinged upon and influenced developments in North and South America. Without the French alliance of 1778, for example, America's War of Independence would not have succeeded. Not only did French men, money, ships, and arms make a difference, but Great Britain's worries about Spain, Russia, and the Netherlands kept it preoccupied in Europe and around its empire in the West Indies and India. For Great Britain, without imperial sovereignty there would be no empire. At the same time, Enlightenment ideas made their way to South America via commerce to influence independence movements on that continent. Then there's the most critical event in world history for the late 18th century, with continuing ramifications well into the 19th century – the French Revolution of 1789.

## BEYOND SLAVERY AGAIN

While there would have been no Civil War in America without slavery, this is not to say that it was the sole or single cause of that conflict either in the form of proslavery (to perpetuate it and maintain the South as a white man's land) or as anti-slavery (in defense of black freedom and equality). Racism was truly an American phenomenon in the 19th century and not confined to the South alone or to Democrats in the North. Anti-slavery advocates (colonizers and early slavery restrictionists) along with Garrisonian immediate abolitionists and the Republican party of 1854-60 all expressed racist views. Lincoln was no racial egalitarian even as he was re-defining the Declaration of Independence to be about equality and issuing the Emancipation Proclamations.

In the end, the immediate issue that led to civil war in America was that of slavery in the territories. At bottom, the territorial question was one ultimately about the Constitution and the nature of the union formed way back in 1787-88. Was it a federal and limited government as a new union of the states or was it a national or "consolidated" and unlimited with the states united under the absolute sovereignty of one single government for all of America? As a local concern, the institution of slavery was very much a state matter to legislate for or against. This is where the founders and framers left it by the rights reserved to the states not specifically delegated to the general or federal government, the concerns of which were limited to mutual affairs. By sovereign states alone had slavery been abolished or allowed.

This remained the Southern constitutional view between 1787-88 and 1860-61 as a matter of principle and the basis of their rejection both of "popular sovereignty" and "total prohibition." States were the foundation of America's extended republic and as such they alone had the final authority to decide for slavery or not, even if the likely outcome was anti-slavery and free-soil. The federal and limited nature of the constitution and the union had a greater significance beyond the momentary issues of the day, including slavery. The future was very much on the mind of Southern politicos as well as the present.

The South was not asserting state sovereignty as something new, as argued by Arthur E. Bestor Jr. Calhoun's insistence on sovereignty indivisible, moreover, was not a later innovation either. The myth here is that of "divided sovereignty" popularized by mainstream Constitutional authorities Charles E. Merriman and Andrew C. McLaughlin. The revolution that was America's War of Independence is to be found in the transferring of sovereignty from government to the people – of the states. America's founders and framers only divided the powers of government between a general authority and the states in keeping with *imperium in imperio*. This colonial demand for local rule within an imperial structure, rejected by Great Britain, became the foundation for the rights of states. A federal government as a confederacy served its purposes well for a long time. One single government over all was "monarchy." True Whigs as republicans and federalists at the Founding not only demanded equal state representation in the Senate, but persisted in the demand for constitutional amendments to secure individual liberties and the rights of states. Thus the Constitution of 1787-88 as amended with the Bill of Rights, a confederate government. America would be a union of the states rather than a united state. More important, slavery and freedom could co-exist pending the gradual and peaceable abolition of the former that dispersal into the territories was intended to help accomplish.

## LINCOLN, 1854, AND 1776

The question remains, however, regarding the revival of "free soilism" after the Kansas-Nebraska Acts of 1854. Slavery based on plantation agriculture was not about to expand to any greater extent than the "Natural Limits" of geography, climate, and soil imposed on staple crop production, especially cotton (absent modern irrigation technology). The Missouri Compromise, moreover, was recognized (in keeping with "Natural Limits") that territory above 36° 30' would likely become free soil by more Northern than Southern settlement.

The new Republican Party's slogan of "Free Soil, Free Labor, and Free Men" meant no blacks at all in the territories. This was their non-negotiable demand for a total prohibition of slavery from the territories by unilateral Congressional or national authority! "Popular sovereignty" (as advocated by Sen. Stephen A. Douglas) and Southern "state sovereignty" were alike rejected because both policies accepted slavery as a right rather than the absolute and moral wrong it was. (Romantic perfectionism again! On this point, Stewart Winger's *Lincoln, Religion, and Romantic Cultural Politics* [DeKalb, Illinois, 2003] is most instructive.) To them, America had to cease being half slave and half free. Whereas the abolitionists' Romantic perfectionism lacked any nationalist element, this Lincoln and the Republicans provided by their reinterpretation of the Declaration of Independence not only to be about the promise of equal rights for all men, but also as the charter of a national and unified government superior to the Constitution. Garrison and his followers, it needs to be remembered, were decidedly anti-statist and anarchical. Garrison, of course, famously dismissed the authority of the Constitution as a "proslavery compact" and "a Covenant with Death"!

Despite the inherent racism of "Free Soil, Free Labor, and Free Men," Lincoln and the Republicans were able to mute and deflect the egalitarian aspect of the appeal to the Declaration of Independence. This was accomplished by an ingenious shift in argument to focus the debate on the future of slavery in America. With their white supporters assured about maintaining the North as a white man's land, attention could be diverted to the South itself. As long as slavery persisted there, so too would an ideology of inequality and subservience.

With Lincoln in particular leading the way, Republicans began to emphasize the denial by Democrats, North and South, of the "glittering generalities" about the rights of man that they believed informed the American founders at the birth of the republic. Their collective rejection thus became proof of a retrogression from the ideals of the founders. The proslavery argument, the denial of equality in favor of inequality, could easily be portrayed as a threat to infiltrate the North and endanger free labor there!

Here was the national threat that slavery posed and that required a new policy of non-extension by total prohibition. By 1860, building upon arguments Lincoln perfected in his famous debates with Stephen A. Douglas, the idea of a "Slave Power" gained momentum and credence. So, too, did a conviction beyond anti-extensionism that America had to cease being half slave and half free. In Lincoln's words: "I believe this government cannot endure permanently, half slave and half free. I do not expect the Union to be dissolved; I do not expect the house to fall; but I do expect it will cease to be divided. It will become all one thing, or all the other." (Lincoln to Oliver P. Hall and others, February 4, 1860, in Basler, *Writings and Speeches*, 109-110.)

The nationalist imperative that inspired Lincoln and the Republicans was influenced by the revolutions of 1848 in Europe, or rather the failure of these revolutions to achieve liberal or radical reforms or unification. If the forces of conservatism and reaction were reasserting themselves in Europe, so too was the advance of slavery and the "Slave Power" in America as events between 1850 and 1860 seemed to demonstrate. Repeatedly, between 1854 and 1860, did Lincoln and the Republicans refer to an "Irrepressible Conflict" between freedom and slavery that was also part of a larger on-going struggle in Europe between believers in the "axioms of free society (associated with Jefferson and his Declaration) and those seeking to supplant "the principles of free government, and restoring those of classification, caste, and legitimacy." Citing those in America, North and South, who denied the supposed principles of Jefferson, Lincoln declared: "One dashingly calls them 'glittering generalities'; another calls them 'self evident lies'; and still others insidiously argue that they apply only to the 'superior races' .... "These expressions, differing in form, are identical in object and effect" that "would delight a convocation of crowned heads, plotting against the people." These "are the van-guard – the miners, and sappers – of returning despotism. We must repulse them, or they will subjugate us."

Very much in Romantic and perfectionist terms, Lincoln continued. "This is a world of compensations; and he who would be no slave, must consent to have no slave. Those who deny freedom to others, deserve it not for themselves; and, under a just God, cannot long retain it." Then, reinterpreting Jefferson to make him one of them, and his Declaration to mean what it did not, Lincoln called the American Revolution *a struggle for national independence by a single people.*" (Italics added) "All honor to Jefferson – to the man who, in the concrete pressure [of the times] ... had the coolness, forecast, and capacity to introduce into a merely revolutionary document an abstract truth, applicable to all men and all times, and so to embalm it there, that to-day, and in all coming days, it shall be a rebuke and a stumbling- block to the very harbingers of re-appearing tyranny and oppression." (Lincoln to Henry L. Pierce and others, *Writings and Speeches*, April 6, 1859, 18-19.)

A new party was needed to arrest the spread of despotism here, beginning with restricting the spread of slavery into the territories. Transforming the Declaration of Independence into a "sacred document" with egalitarian and nationalist intentions beyond those of the founders and framers, while serving to link the Republicans to the principles of 1776 and 1787 (by deliberate misinterpretation), still left intact the Southern claim to be the real heirs of the founders and framers. Something else was needed to challenge this assertion. The perception of the South had to be changed from positive (republican and constitutional) to negative (slavery as its central theme and as an aggressive "Slave Power"). By 1860, the myths of democracy and a reactionary South were fully developed to influence the important presidential election of that year and change the course of American history — to a crisis of the union about more than slavery alone.

With reference to events in Europe, Timothy Roberts in *Distant Revolutions: 1848 and the Challenge to American Exceptionalism* (Charlottesville and London: University of Virginia Press, 2009) concludes that the failed revolution of 1848 "bolstered the case for American exceptionalism."

> Many Americans consoled themselves that despite problems emerging in American politics and society over slavery, there was no chance that a violent European-style revolution against legal authority could or should occur in the United States. But over the course of the 1850s, this situation changed, driven by the question of slavery's expansion, which soon fragmented American politics. The problem of slavery, as well as, eventually, the Civil War itself, likely would have developed in America even without

the 1848 revolutions. But the way that the American
republic became unstable in the 1850s owed to
antislavery Americans' perception that conditions in
America had become foreign and alien – similar to
conditions in Europe in 1848-1852 – and therefore
were particularly dangerous. The growing crisis thus
needed to be dealt with outside the traditional
political compromise that the American Revolution
allegedly had bequeathed. (*Distant Revolutions*, 15)

Continuing, he writes that

the 1848 revolutions undermined faith in American
'exemplarism' – the belief that America should merely
preserve its status as a global model .... The 1848
revolutions did not by themselves cause the Civil War,
but they did contribute to its timing and its meaning
for many Americans. (*Ibid.*, 20)

Territorial acquisitions in the 1840s precipitated a sectional
Political alignment. Outbreaks of violence in the West, a symptom
of the that alignment, became significant partly because a growing
number of Americans came to interpret violence – a form of
Revolutionary 'righteous violence' ... as signaling how America
should become more like revolutionary Europe, rather than the
other way around. Thus, I maintain that the role of revolutionary
events in Europe directed Americans' path to the Civil War.
America's ultimate response to the 1848 revolutions. The United
States and Europe were drawn closer together, not in the way
anticipated by Americans who in 1848 professed faith in
American exemplarism, "but through shared experiences of
nation-building through violence." (*Ibid.*, 20)

Moderate as Lincoln was as an antislavery advocate, he too
(like John Brown and Henry David Thoreau and other radicals)
saw "the Republican Party as part of a transatlantic liberal
movement, because its ascension to power and the Southern

secession that his election precipitated would create the opportunity to save American republicanism .... Lincoln committed to stop the secession movement because he, like other Republican spokesmen, had been both inspired and embarrassed by events in Hungary and elsewhere in Europe a decade before antislavery forces gained power in the United States. He thus became committed to consolidating American power, even at great human sacrifice, so that the country might fulfill its role as a global model .... The Europeans Kossuth and Mazzini had argued for a right of revolution. As their American counterpart, Lincoln ultimately enforced the same right, for the same purpose. As the careers of the Hungarian, the Italian, and the American attest, history does not show popularly accountable government being achieved or sustained without significant violence." (*Ibid.*, 189-190)

Lincoln's pronouncements about a country ceasing to be half slave and half free, shared by Republicans, were in effect a declaration of war against South since slavery could not be separated from its immense and longstanding integration with the daily life of the South as well as its economic and ideological bases of support. All that awaited for a civil war to occur was the capture of the federal government by the new Republican Party, which is what happened in 1860. The Southern view of Republicans as "fanatics," "Jacobins," and "black republicans" was by no means an exaggeration in the context of world history since 1789. Representing as it did the end of the old republic as a federal union of the states, the South proceeded to withdraw from the union in 1860-61, citing the right of revolution contained in the Declaration of Independence. Referring to the same historical document, Lincoln and the Republicans denied the right of secession as the *ultimo ratio* on the part of the South. And the Civil

War of Northern-Romantic-Perfectionist-Nationalist origins began.

Far from preserving the Union as they claimed to be doing, Lincoln and the Republicans were very much about remaking it anew. Although couched in the language of the founders and framers, their principles of 1776 and 1787 now embodied not original intentions but very different ones informed by 19th century Romantic-nationalist philosophy. It was not the South that changed but the North (or a dominant part of it). Nor did the South reject the ideas and ideals of the founding generation. Rather the principles of 1776 and 1787 were reinterpreted by the North to be more democratic, egalitarian, abolitionist, and nationalist than they really were. Revolutions have to be justified, of course, and this is what Lincoln and the Republicans accomplished with their new history for a new nation in the making between 1815 and 1865.

For the South, the sudden rise of a new Republican Party to national prominence between 1854 and 1860 and succeeding in getting Abraham Lincoln elected as 16th president, signaled more than the end of the old republic and secession as an essential right of self-government. By their reinterpretation of 1776 in egalitarian and nationalist terms, Lincoln and the Republicans also belied their rhetoric of respecting the Constitution and not interfering with slavery where it was legally protected. Southerners knew better. They also knew their history, American, European, and ancient.

# ABOUT THE AUTHOR

WALTER KIRK WOOD holds a Ph.D. from the University of South Carolina. He retired after a long career as Professor of History at Alabama State University (1986-2010) and now resides in Lexington, South Carolina. He is the author of many scholarly articles and of *Nullification: A Constitutional History, 1776 – 1833*, 2 vols.

# AVAILABLE FROM SHOTWELL PUBLISHING

If you enjoyed this book, perhaps some of our other titles will pique your interest. The following titles are now available at Amazon and all major online retailers. Enjoy!

JOYCE BENNETT

- *Maryland, My Maryland: The Cultural Cleansing of a Small Southern State*

JERRY BREWER

- *Dismantling the Republic*

ANDREW P. CALHOUN, JR.

- *My Own Darling Wife: Letters From a Confederate Volunteer [John Francis Calhoun]*

JOHN CHODES

- *Segregation: Federal Policy or Racism?*
- *Washington's KKK: The Union League During Southern Reconstruction*

PAUL C. GRAHAM

- *Confederaphobia: An American Epidemic*
- *When the Yankees Come: Former South Carolina Slaves Remember Sherman's Invasion* (Voices from the Dust I)

JOSEPH JAY

- *Sacred Conviction: The South's Stand for Biblical Authority*

JAMES R. KENNEDY

- *Dixie Rising: Rules for Rebels*

JAMES R. & WALTER D. KENNEDY

- *Punished with Poverty: The Suffering South*
- *Yankee Empire: Aggressive Abroad and Despotic At Home*

PHILIP LEIGH

- *The Devil's Town: Hot Spring During the Gangster Era*

MICHAEL MARTIN

- *Southern Grit: Sensing the Siege at Petersburg*

LEWIS LIBERMAN

- *Snowflake Buddies: ABCs for Leftism for Kids!*

CHARLES T. PACE

- *Lincoln As He Was*
- *Southern Independence. Why War?*

JAMES RUTLEDGE ROESCH

- *From Founding Fathers to Fire Eaters: The Constitutional Doctrine of States' Rights in the Old South*

Kirkpatrick Sale

+ *Emancipation Hell: The Tragedy Wrought By Lincoln's Emancipation Proclamation*

Karen Stokes

+ *A Legion of Devils: Sherman in South Carolina*
+ *Carolina Love Letters*

John Vinson

+ *Southerner, Take Your Stand!*

Howard Ray White

+ *Understanding Creation and Evolution*

Clyde N. Wilson

+ *Annals of the Stupid Party: Republicans Before Trump* (The Wilson Files 3)
+ *Lies My Teacher Told Me: The True History of the War for Southern Independence*
+ *Nullification: Reclaiming Consent of the Governed* (The Wilson Files 2)
+ *The Old South: 50 Essential Books* (Southern Reader's Guide I)
+ *The Yankee Problem: An American Dilemma* (The Wilson Files 1)

---

## Green Altar Books (Literary Imprint)
RANDALL IVEY

- *A New England Romance & Other SOUTHERN Stories*

JAMES EVERETT KIBLER

- *Tiller (Clay Bank County, IV)*

KAREN STOKES

- *Belles: A Carolina Romance*
- *Honor in the Dust*
- *The Immortals*
- *The Soldier's Ghost: A Tale of Charleston*

---

## GOLD-BUG (Mystery & Suspense Imprint)
MICHAEL ANDREW GRISSOM

- *Billie Jo*

BRANDI PERRY

- *Splintered: A New Orleans Tale*

MARTIN L. WILSON

- *To Jekyll and Hide*

# Free Book Offer

Sign-up for new release notification and receive a FREE downloadable edition of *Lies My Teacher Told Me: The True History of the War for Southern Independence* by Dr. Clyde N. Wilson by visiting <u>FreeLiesBook.com</u> or by texting the word "Dixie" to 345-345. You can always unsubscribe and keep the book, so you've got nothing to lose!

**SOUTHERN WITHOUT APOLOGY**

Made in the USA
Monee, IL
21 November 2021

82520035R00049